NO CONTACT, NO NARC

30 WAYS TO MAINTAIN NO CONTACT, STAY AWAY FROM THE
NARCISSIST IN YOUR LIFE, AND BREAK THE CYCLE OF ABUSE.

By L.W. Hawksby, author of bestseller *Dangerous Normal
People. Understanding Casanova Psychopaths and The
Narcissistic Virus*

"A narcissist has many nightmares; You, rising after the abuse.
You, becoming well and happy after the abuse. You, meeting
someone else, you ignoring the narc's baiting, you forgetting the
abuse enough to move on and love again, and you moving on to
have a better life than before you even met the narc"

L.W. Hawksby

2023

About The Author

Glossary of Terms

Introduction

So, you've bought this book to help you maintain NC (No Contact), and stay the heck away from someone who has narcissistically abused you *and* finally gone too far? So far that finally you WANT them gone? And to not come back?

If so, one thing I can say with 100% confidence before we even get started is you are already amazing and well on your way to cancelling out that twonk of a person, and subsequently getting your life back. Because with No Contact there is, quite literally, No Narc.

NC is the ONLY WAY you can "buy some time" and start the recovery and realisation process regarding what has happened to you. No matter what, you must accept NC and maintain it in the very early stages of your departure from this horrendous relationship. It may be unpopular, if you share a child or children, you can (at least) for a short time stop child contact to preserve your sanity and rebuild your emotional wellbeing.

This guidebook is not about Grey Rock, because Grey Rock is not quite as effective, and it is not ideal once you have first ended an NPD Abuse relationship. You can do Grey Rock (if needs be) once your No Contact mindset is solid. Grey Rock is for people legally or financially bound to their Narcissist or if perhaps your Narc is a parent, and you just can't abandon them.

Now, before we really get into the 30 tips I have to share with you, I'll give you a little bit of background as to who I am, and why I consider myself the No Contact Queen.

In late March 2016, I gave my worst Narcissist (whom I call Narc2) an ultimatum. I had already pretty much tried everything to calm him down, make him drug-free and stop him cheating and, of course, because he is a Narcissist, these failed, and I was abused even worse each time I failed in both Grey Rock and No Contact.

(This book may trigger you, as I will share personal examples of the Narcissistic Personality Disorder Abuse I suffered and others have suffered, so please be mindful to step away from reading, reach out to a calming influence and reboot before coming back to No Contact, No Narc, if you feel emotional overwhelm or an urge to self-harm or indulge in negative self-soothing behaviours in any way)

The ultimatum for Narc2 was that if he were prepared to attend rehab, and stop doing all the awful things he so enjoyed, I would be prepared to continue the relationship and do so with forgiveness. This ultimatum resulted in a few minutes of silence (Oh, those dammed WhatsApp blue tics!) then a tirade of abuse including projection, deflection and blame shifting. *(Don't worry, I will do a glossary of terms at the rear of this handbook, but you can always learn 112 of them by buying **Dangerous Normal People**, anyway... wink wink!)*

Narc2 then blocked me (for the squillionth time in 2½ years) and I resolved that this was it. The end! No way was I going to be a doormat anymore! Not a chance. He could absolutely jog on! Go and continue his nonsense and abuse all those women and girls I kept finding out about. I was done! It was over! Finito! I decided that HE was dumped. I felt powerful and had a warped sense of happy at that moment.

Of course, I knew nothing about Narcissists and No Contact, or even enough about myself to help me maintain my "sobriety" from him and his Flying Monkeys. I managed to stay NC and not message or call him for almost a week. Big wow, a week?!

In between times I obsessively watched my Narc's social media and the other women he was engaging with, too. They would block and unblock me, post things that would make anyone's toes curl and trigger even Mother Theresa into getting a gun licence. But, as you soon will learn, this is how Narcs and *their* Narcs (and even just new supplies) behave after a victim has been discarded or started NC.

To cut a long story short (because I wrote over 250 pages on it in *Dangerous Normal People*, and a bit in *The Forgivers Club* too) I ended up losing almost a stone in weight, although I already had a BMI of 19, and weighed around 7½ stones anyway, lost my sense of taste and smell (pre-Covid this was scary a.f!) and set about drinking as though all alcohol was about to be destroyed in some sort of booze-thirsty-Zombie apocalypse. Essentially, I went bonkers, and self-harming and self-isolation were all I could muster the energy for.

Cue classic Narcissistic Post-Separation Hoovering (yes, this will be in the glossary!) and as I started to take the first steps away from the Trauma Bond, and dared to post online that I had a male friend coming to visit to try and make me eat, Narc2 broke his own NC with an intimate image, and a request to see me the next day. By now we were in late April, and our NC had lasted three to four weeks.

Absolutely shattered, confused, but still addicted to my abuser and my desperate search for the pain of the break-up to end, and for him to give in to my request for "fixing" himself as I'd asked before, I let him visit me in my home the next morning.

Without going into the details in *Dangerous Normal People*, I can tell you that something most purists would call rape happened. Certainly sexual assault. At best Sexual Coercion. Not that there is a "best" scenario to be found when Narcissists return to their victims for sex, only to make it clear that we are to be set aside as supply, while the new fresh supply or Narc Ex still thinks they are *The One* for the shared Narcissist.

I knew then, as he trotted happily down my stairs to go "to the gym" (aka go and have sex with some new poor wee soul at the gym) and looked up at me with those dark, satisfied and gleeful eyes of a well-fed predator, that I had made the worst mistake of my entire life, letting him into my home and body. I knew then I f***ed up royally.

Much more happened after that, although I did not break NC with Narc2 directly (he tried to break it many times over the years though), I attempted to contact anyone else I thought could give me closure and forgiveness. Those people saw this as unlawful contact and, well, the rest is in my police file!

Because I had become very, very unwell during that particular NPD Abuse relationship, my behaviour and choices while struggling with the aftermath of the abuse, *and* my lack of knowledge on Narcissists and how they often make their victims very like them. I did some terrible things that summer of 2016.

So NC for me was a mess! I did not do it properly, I did not use it to my advantage, and I did not stop sexually and socially engaging with abusive people. In fact, I ran at them as though they were giant vats of Baileys-flavoured ice-cream. And the next couple of years were the worst in my life, and in my children's lives.

So this book feels important, for me and people like me. I will mostly focus on NC after an NPD abuse relationship of the sexual kind, but will throw in some examples of NC in regard to abusive friends, family members, and colleagues also. The NC tips here can be adapted to your specific needs, as I have written them in my simple and classic no-frills style.

Lastly, before we begin your NC journey, you will see there is a lot of space at the bottom of some pages. This is so you can make notes, write down your own personal experience or feelings using the tips I give you, and even just follow the instructions and write down the things which work well for you, alongside the tip on that particular page. When coaching my No Contact clients, I can be quite bossy, but it really is tough LOVE, so this book may read like a workbook at times – you'll thank me later!

"How you'll feel soon; Reborn. Contented. Bold. Safe. Optimistic. Calm. Hopeful. Fresh. New. Proud. Enlightened. Lovable. Whole. Worthy. Driven. Focused. Yourself."

L.W. Hawksby

Chapter 1

Let's talk about ways NC is broken by the Narcissist.

Narcissists like to have supply, a LOT of supply. They need it, in fact. One supply source or even a handful is rare. These disordered people have so many gaps in their personality and so many issues, that human supply is necessary for them to feel they are not only existing, but that they are safe and even "doing well" in life.

Many victims will be "done" with a Narc, and go NC successfully, and the Narc will mourn and rage at the "loss" for a while, but only until a new fresh supply arrives or succumbs, and the Narc is fine again. Think of Narcs and supplies as a game of chess. As long as you are in the game (in CONTACT) you are a supply of some sort.

So, Narcs can break NC with you in many ways, but they will choose the easiest, least messy, least easy to prove, and the most successful methods. As you may know now, Narcs like no mess, and lots of success! No drama, but to be central in the diorama. Lots of fuel, with no actual... I can't think of what word to use but you get my drift.

1. Hoovering: This is when an abuser contacts a victim directly with false apologies, platitudes, compliments, songs, long messages, flattery, renewed future faking and pretty much loads of chat saying they are sorry and will change, so you let them suck you back into the relationship.

2. Hoovering by proxy: Same as above but using someone else as the vessel of this crap. Usually a shared friend or even one of

yours. Some Narcs use grown-up children to do this. Ugh.

3. Triangulation: The Narc showing off a new supply or ex (this is common) and making you feel so crap, you want the Narc back so you are more open to Hoovering or will even apologise and Hoover the Narc yourself. Narcs will also get new supplies or exes (who they are sleeping with) to contact a victim to ping info and or abuse back and forth to keep the drama and chaos going. The Perp, the Victim, the Enabler. A classic "triangle" that is only broken by NC!

4. Passive Hoovering: This is very covert. The Narc posts memes, old pictures of you both, hints that only you – the victim – will be emotionally triggered and affected by. Posting social media statuses of them at your fave restaurant or even going on holiday to a place important to you both.

5. The "Whoopsadaisy" Hoover. When a Narc texts you, calls you, emails you, or tags you and, when you reply, states "that was a mistake!" or "I must have sat on my phone!" or "Who is this?!" to get you to respond, or keep replying out of agitation and confusion and even anger. You know it wasn't a mistake... or was it?

6. The "I hope you are well, how are you?" bland and random reach-out (of any type) when you are either doing really badly (so extra vulnerable after a recent setback that they found out about) or doing really well and are in a new relationship, fresh dating, got new hair, bought a house or moved jobs. Again, this is simply to be a part of your life and rattle you, to have you thinking back and consider breaking your NC.

7. The fake apology. OMG, this is huge! A Narc has learned how to fake contrition, sadness, and regret. They do this to maintain supply for longer than any other abuser could. It is pure

manipulation. But Narcs know we need apologies. That it is all we live for both in and after the abusive relationship. We hope above all hopes that they mean it "this time". But they never do. It is baiting and breadcrumbing and cruel.

8. The "I'm not well. I need you. I had an accident" crap. This is also very very common. Especially if your Narc was an addict, or known for breakdowns, meltdowns, relapses, self-harming or binges. They set you up to respond to this right at the start. "I have depression, so I won't always be ok" they say. "I sometimes get ill; will you always be there for me?" they whine.

9. The " You've really let me down. My family miss you" Hoover. They lay guilt on you because you are no longer involved in the family around the Narc. Whether you discarded the Narc, or they discarded you, this is a useful tool. You will immediately feel bad for Nana Pat or Papa Jo or Aunty Alison and the nephews and that one decent Christmas you had or that not-too-bad weekend away. Once you re-enter the family and hope the Narc sees how loyal you are, the abuse will start again, and the family will be told you harassed the Narc to get let "back in".

There will be a lot of other Hoover techniques, and I encourage you to note down any particularly brazen or shocking ones here.

"I am not who I was when I was in trauma. You are who you are because you cause trauma. I would rather be me.
All day long."
L.W. Hawksby

This space is for you.

Chapter 2

Let's talk about ways NC is broken by you, the victim.

Reverse Hoovering is a thing. I did it, a lot. I still feel the shame of it. I will never get over it. But I do understand it. And that helps a lot. By understanding it, I am in a good position to explain it to you and help you avoid it or forgive yourself if you have already done it.

Reverse Hoovering is when you give in to the fear, loneliness and panic of being NC with your Narc or when you sense they are about to discard or go NC with you.

In abusive relationships with Narcissists, they pretty much teach us how to read their moods, so we can mitigate against them and protect ourselves from any tantrums/abuse/outbursts/etc that we have learned to expect.

Of course, Narcs move the goalposts and no matter how hard we try to soothe and calm and fawn for the Narc, they almost always still abuse or discard us. Which is why "walking on eggshells" is so common.

Those of us who have been brought up in chaotic households or have natural fawning and caring qualities (and, dare I say, co-dependency issues) will very quickly learn that even when we are out of favour with a Narc (and they have gone NC with us) if We Hoover the Narc with our own platitudes, apologies, self-flagellation, promises of change and fawning, the NC means nothing as the Narc will give in to our pressure and their own need for us.

This is Reverse Hoovering. And trust me, accepting that we did this is very, very hard. So my advice is more of a warning. Please don't do it. The Narc will use this against you and say you are the stalker, and harasser, and weak, and an addict etc.

We can also break NC ourselves if we post stuff about the Narc online – screenshots, memes, pics, or rants. We are still (trust me) communicating with the Narc. Deep down we do it to try and upset them and shame them and guilt-trip them, and we hope that the Narc will see it and suddenly feel this overwhelm of shame and beg us to come back. Be honest with yourself. And please do not do this. I cover how to avoid this later.

This space is for you.

Chapter 3

World's briefest summary of why Narcs do what they do, and why NC is the only option right now.

Long title, short answer? Mainly because this is not an NPD abuse or Narcissist guidebook, it is a No Contact workbook. But also because this is my fourth book on Narcs (the best one that really explains them in intimate relationships is four times the size of this, and you can find it on Amazon!) and there are many YouTubers and authors who write about Narcs, but not many who focus on just maintaining No Contact.

But to help make this book as educational as I can, here is a brief explanation of why Narcs do what they do, and why this has happened to you at least once.

Narcissistic Personality Disorder is a Cluster B personality disorder. It sits within a group of fixed mental health illnesses (the jury is out on that) apparently but, unlike MH issues, it is not manageable and cannot be effectively medicated or healed.

At some point, the person with NPD has had trauma or perceived trauma from abuse, neglect, spoiling, or all of the above. The child or young person develops through these negative experiences and learns how to "play" the victim, play dead, manipulate, shout back, bully, walk away, dissociate, use and abuse and kick-off whenever they feel "unsafe" or not in control. Throw in sexual (and other important) relationships, and the person is now legally an adult but stunted still in their childhood wounds and ways. They are also now very angry at the world, so have little to no empathy for other people who they perceive as more attractive or luckier or smarter than they are – this is why they target people they can use to "be better" or "look better".

So, all this considered, the Narc has to lie and manipulate and take, take, take and deny, deny, deny in order to feel that they not only exist, but that they are "doing well". Human beings become supply to their needs, and the Narc as they age, gets better and better at getting supply and getting rid of supply. Hence the love bombing, devaluation and discard cycles they use.

There is SO MUCH more to this and honestly, I would love you to read up on it! However, it doesn't take a genius to know you are best off not engaging with Narcs at all, but they are masters at winning supply and this book is about the No Contact lifestyle and me helping you stop your supply line to your Narc and not becoming a supply to them or anyone else ever again.

"It doesn't matter if they (other people) believe you. Because each little piece of evidence fingerprints their minds. They will not forget what you say. Even if they deny the power of it right now."

L.W. Hawksby

This space is for you.

Chapter 4

30 Tips to maintain No Contact

I have not structured these tips in any particular order because NPD abuse victims (and domestic abuse victims who keep returning to their abuser) do not really follow a set pattern of recovery needs. We all need different levels of information and support to understand why No Contact is so important, and why we must must must maintain it, especially in the earliest days of our healing.

One of these tips might just hit you like a train and solve whatever issue you have in staying Narc-free. Or you may decide to use a handful! I hope you use all 30, whenever you need them. Narcs have so many tricks up their sleeves to make us weaken and react or go back to the abuse that you may well need a few of these tricks of your own, to stay strong and silent, which drives abusers and stalkers absolutely potty!

Tip 1

The Pen is Mightier Than a Machete

The Trauma Bond is a very real, very confusing and very painful collection of feelings, behaviours and schemas, that your Narc created between and around you, to make sure that NC would always feel impossible.

So you need to "cut" the bond, in order to accept your NC status and begin the process of deleting that Narc and that relationship from your life.

For me, and perhaps for you, the Trauma Bond began right at the start of the relationship. My Narc2 was exceptional at reading (using cognitive empathy) and mirroring me. He made my attraction to him and our (fake) future together extra tasty with vast reams of messages, songs and, of course, compliments. Narcs know we need validation and to feel worthy and attractive, and they give us these things smoothly as though we are soulmates who have finally found each other.

A big part of the Trauma Bond is how we fantasise and obsess over all the "good stuff" from the start. From what is called The Love Bombing Stage. There is also a stage before this, called the Idealization Stage. Both these stages are grooming. Full stop.

Your Narc was never ever that person, everything they said was designed to draw you in AND hook you. This was the first tendril of the Trauma Bond, quietly and insidiously wrapping themselves around you tightly, but tying you to the Narc, too.

The physical pain of not being around, near, or in favour with, my Narc, was intense! I know you have felt it, too. This squeezing and jabbing of the heart is like a heart attack, but over and over again as it hits you over and over again that "the love of your life" is no longer in your life! It's over. It's done. It was all for nothing. They don't love you! How could they do this? This is not real. They are pretending. The new love (the new supply) stole them! You can get back to "the way it was" and start over!

Now, now, now! Stop! See all that wishful thinking, self-gaslighting, toxic hope and belief that your Narc is actually a nice person corrupted by life or a new supply and they really love you but need a break or space or to see you in agony, yadda yadda? It is total bull. It is your Trauma Bond squeezing and squeezing the rational side of your brain, and tugging and pulling on the irrational side of your brain, and the person holding those strings is an abuser and most likely a cheat, too.

All the obsessive thoughts about "the good times" in the past and the "plans we had for the future" are clouding what really matters; what happened in the middle. In the Devaluation Stage. So we are going to list the crappy, vile and evil things this person has SAID and DONE, after the flattery and great sex and gifts, and BEFORE the amazing things you both decided your shared future holds.

Every time you feel that shard of glass slice through your heart, or that invisible grip of shock and disappointment squeeze your jaw into a full-on clench, or that cold wave of humiliation and confusion sweep across your whole body, I want you to write down at least one horrid devaluation event on a piece of paper.

You can write it here! You can write it big. You can write it over and over. And you absolutely can dig deep and write as many as you can remember. AND you can come back here and add new events/abuses in, as your Mind Fog lifts, and you hear more and more bad news that your Narc hid from you or is getting up to now.

Read over what you have written. Read it aloud. Share it with your closest friend or an adult child. Anyone who hates the Narc who is there for you.

Listing the actual, real, truthful things your Narc said and did will drag you (kicking and screaming) back to reality. Because the Trauma Bond is built on lies. You need reality right now. You need reminders of what has REALLY happened to you, and not the crap your Narc spouted to manipulate you and make excuses for abusing you.

This space is for you.

Tip 2

Who Are You?

Toxic people such as Narcissists choose targets and make them victims through a conscious process of watching you, covertly stalking you, obsessing over you and using cognitive empathy. By the time the devaluation starts, and not before, the Narcissist studies you so well that they know you better than you know yourself.

Narcissists do not choose mentally healthy, balanced, strong and proud people. Whether you like it or not, your Narcissist chose you for your supply (usually positive things like being attractive, well off/financially secure, your generosity, your social skills/social status, your tenderness, and your optimism) BUT THEY GET INTO YOUR WORLD (and body) by spotting and then using your flaws.

I prefer to call these the "chinks in your armour" rather than flaws, but Narcs think differently. They don't see chinks or cute little vulnerabilities, they see flaws that they can exaggerate, manipulate, and later destroy you for. Think of a vampire victim – the Vampire almost always gets its teeth into a bared, naked, stretched neck. Narcs are the same, they see that wide open area to feed from, and they go for it. But not before they are absolutely sure that this vulnerability exists.

How do they know that you will fall for their charms and open up your blood supply to them? They test you. And that way the chinks in your armour are confirmed. Narcs like to be careful and do due diligence. Especially the Casanova Psychopath types and Covert types.

So, think back to when you met your Narc. How did they know you were "up for it"? What did they ask? What did they share with you, to make you share back? What did you tell them about yourself or your past that they were able to feed on?

Narcs are looking for people who "fake" certain personality traits. They look for those of us in unhappy relationships, who are sexually dissatisfied, who have low to moderate self-esteem, who pretend to be confident, and who are trying to better ourselves or push on to have a better life. None of these things are bad but, to a Narc, they are openings of opportunity!

These traits mean the Narc can mirror us with "me too" conspiratorially, and pretend to be equally ambitious and vulnerable using Mirroring. These traits also let the Narc know that they can pretend to fill these gaps with the right words and promises, making us feel whole, content, and bonded. Remember that line "You Complete Me" – that's what a Narcissistic Abuser wants you to say and feel about them.

The Narcissist also wants to use these weaknesses against you, and not just "cover them up" with their flattery and promises. The Narc wants a victim to have low self-esteem so that you will put up with more abuse than someone with high esteem.

The chinks in your armour are what make your boundaries weak. And these let a Narc into your world.

Now, to my tip on how to use this knowledge.

I would like you to write down what parts of your personality and life you shared with the person who later became your abuser. Be honest with yourself. But also read them back, and realise that a person who "loves" you, who you were fantasising about making up with or contacting a few pages ago, actually groomed you and used you, over and above knowing you were already vulnerable. This is an ABUSER. Never ever forget the person you long to break NC with, is an ABUSER. They were one when they met you, and they are even better at it now they have destroyed you. You were a practice range. You handed them the weapon and stood there wide open.

Aahhhh, see that? That anger you feel? It feels better than grief and loss and regret, doesn't it?! Good. NC relies on that. The more regret you feel, the more likely you are to break NC and try to unregret yourself for getting away from your Narc.

This space is for you.

Tip 3

Allow Anger & Gain Closure

What you are going through is a form of grief. Both personally and professionally, I think it is worse than "normal" grief.

When you lose a loved one who loved you, or an innocent person who never did you any harm, you will feel many emotions across a spectrum and, yes, anger is one of those emotions. Loss of control, regret, unfairness, injustice, and even denial that the person has gone forever is socially acceptable and we are told to embrace them.

But when an abuser leaves our life, discards us or we are forced to discard them, we feel all the same emotions but more intensely. Why? Because chucked in there is the knowledge that the person making you feel all these things (deliberately) is alive and kicking a can-can dance over your "grave"!

To stay NC you need to accept this person is what they deny they are. They are what they claim they hate. They are what your gut says they are (more about this in later chapters) and they are not remotely bothered that they hurt you and destroyed all you were and all you hoped to become, in front of your friends, family, children, exes (ugh) and colleagues.

The Narc is a Narc. You are not the first victim. You won't be the last. They cannot change for two reasons.

1. They do not think they did or do any wrong and blame you for what is now a bloody mess. Often these are Vulnerable Covert Narcs, who have the self-awareness of a packet of fudge. They think they are sweet and innocent and never at fault, even though they can give

you diabetes and love handles.

2. Or they are Overt Narcs. They know they are vile. They revel in it. They feel powerful, safe and in control, knowing they can puppeteer and hurt people over and over again, because they have no regrets, and have no desire to change.

Accepting that your Narc *is* a Narc is absolutely key in staying NC.

Write down all the nasty things your Narc said about other people. How they judged them and called them out and criticised and mocked them. How they promised to change and did not. List all this. Remind yourself with every sentence that the Narc is so deluded and judgemental; to say all these things and still BE what they are is proof they cannot and will not change. If you break NC you are going back to this creature. This HYPOCRITE.

So, no regrets from now on?! Ok! Acceptance is the new you. While we get you past rage and anger and into healing, we can play with your deep, burning, hatred of what has happened to you and what your Narc has done and is doing.

Write down how angry you are. Metaphors, analogies, quotes, anything that represents the anger inside your soul. The anger you want to manifest. What you want to scream in your Narc's face. Get...it...out. This is a safe place, his doorstep or her parents' house living room is not!

Think about the rage. Think about how revved up you feel. How alive you feel. How distracted from boring, useless, cringey, "I wanna contact him/her and say sorry" feelings and fantasies you are. Now, that pain is gonna be your fuel. You are going to harness it and drive yourself forwards into recovery, not reverse backwards into breaking your NC.

Oh, and BTW, if you want to vent your rage at your Narc and maybe his/her new supply, don't. Not only will it prove to everyone (the Narc tells) that you are an angry loon ball who is irrational and harassing/abusing/stalking him, but it is illegal.

To intentionally vent your spleen (however justified) at another person is now a variety of criminal acts. Telecommunications offences, breaches of the peace, stalking, harassment, unwanted contact, all sorts. Emotion is being made illegal so sadly we gotta keep it to ourselves.

Your pain (shown online in socials, in emails, in texts, in voice messages, in replying to same) will make the Narc feel good. Sad, sick, unsavoury, but true. The Narc will show your pain to those they trust to mock you. They will feel "loved". They will feel powerful. They will feel validated. They will know you are so hurt they can Hoover and use you again later.

Part two of this tip adds to closure and acceptance, but it is very, very critical to you not breaking NC.

Almost all of us break NC at the start. Almost all of us accept the Hoovering and let the Narc run over our NC with their Tractor of Twattiness. So let that shit go. BUT once or twice is ok. We can bring you back from that *no problemo*, however... and this is the bad news, and why this book is important: to repeatedly go back to an abuser such as a Narc is to tear the fresh new scar tissue of healing from your flesh and walk back into the fire that burned you. Eventually, you will give up on NC, and succumb to a lifetime of being a sex toy/cash machine/shoulder to cry on/neck to feed from/back-up plan loser. And you won't just lose yourself, you'll lose everyone normal around you and eventually your sanity.

I've seen it several times. I almost did it myself.

What is the second most common reason victims break NC? (By the way, I don't proffer stats for this or links to medical research. I'm not that kind of author or expert. Tough luck. I just go on years and years of experience, too much of it, and speaking to thousands of victims a year.)

The second most common reason victims break NC is to get closure. We need it like oxygen. We fixate on it. We obsess over it. We demand it! "I want answers! Tell me how long!" or "Just at least tell me why?" and classic "Why did you do this to me?" wailing at a Narc's best friend, parent, DMs, answer machine or up at their window like a tragic pigeon without a breadcrumb, is your absolute right. It is natural! BUT, I have to inform you formally at this stage in our relationship, Narcs specifically plan on, choose to, and enjoy your begging. They planned on never ever giving you closure, the moment they started devaluing you. It is just not their thing. They learned a long time ago how it felt good to hear a person beg and beg and beg for something from them. This is their happy place. Their safe place. Confirmation they have harmed you forever and that they have power over you, simply by staying silent.

So, who is going to give you closure (now you've decided to stop breaking NC to try and bully, demand, harass, beg and wheedle it from your Narc and people who know them)?

Before I continue, let me give you some relief. You will see other experts say that closure does not matter, and forgiveness does (more on that later) – they are talking utter twaddle. I have never, ever, said that walking away, questions unanswered, was vaguely easy, comfortable or healing! Never.

I have however experienced incredible moments of relief both in myself and the people I help when they get answers themselves. You just need to stop trying to get that pig to sing, and find a new way to hear the music.

NPDs follow specific patterns. Gender has little to do with it. Age doesn't either. Social class? A little. But in general Narcissistic Personality Disorder and the inevitable abuse that Narcs put victims through is what defines them and makes them predictable. And because they are predictable, smarty pants like me can give you explanations of why they do what they do, and the Narc's answers (usually lies, anyway) are not relevant.

The internet is your oyster. Quora, YouTube, people like me, other victims and survivors and, of course, other books (oof! That hurts!) can give you closure. You can work as hard as you like ticking off those questions that your abuser ignores and refuses to answer. In fact, here you are, with a space to write down some of the most glaringly agonising gaps in your understanding of why a person you loved most in the world has hurt you the most, ever.

Gradually add your answers. Cross off the questions. And give yourself closure, you deserve it.

This space is for you.

Tip 4

Cut Off The Dead Wood

A lot of people forget this bit, and I don't blame you! You are in pain, lonely, frustrated and desperate for company, and maybe still hoping for a little more closure. You may never have been through this before, so you won't know that you MUST go NC with your Narc's closest friends, colleagues, and family. You must.

Blood is thicker than water in almost all instances of any type of drama, crisis or break up. And these people (seeing as they are still hanging about with/putting up with your Narc) have no true idea of the monster in their midst.

Your Narc has hurt people before. Lots of them, probably. And the people around them are enablers, watchers, sympathetic supporters and even hopeful not-yet-supplies and wanna-be-supplies-again. Sad? Yup. Aren't you glad to be out of it?!

The Narc will have hand-picked the best of the worst of these people and made them Flying Monkeys. These people will stalk you, harass you, pretend to be friends with you, and absolutely be all in, FOR THE NARC.

In your vulnerable and desperate state, you won't smell the rats. You will trust them. You will overshare. You will cry and show your scars. You will say things the Narc will regret...

This is why to properly go NC and stay NC, you must delete these people from your life. You may think they are your "shared" contacts and that they are nice, kind, and fair. But when a Narc is cutting through the waters around you, I can assure you, "nice" people become nasty people very quickly, because the Narc is good at grooming, deflecting, playing the victim, and generally getting people to change to suit their needs. They did that to you, so they will have done it to anyone close to them for a long time.

Staying in contact with anyone in the Narc's life may make you feel safe or validated or like you are "winning" the war, but it is not truly authentic or healthy. And you are leaving yourself wide open to either the Narc Hoovering you, or them being able to find out everything about you. This is not true NC.

List everyone you met AFTER you met the Narc via the Narc, and message them. Short and sweet. "Hi. You've heard that blobbymcdickbobfoostyvaj and I (ok, don't use that name. But you can if you want to) have ended. I am not going into detail. I am focusing on me, myself and I, and my healing from what blobbymcdickbobfoostyvaj put me through. With my recovery in mind, I have decided it is healthiest if I have a detox of my socials/phone etc, and you fall into the "I can't trust you fully" category. Bye."

Now, I am half joking, but I think you get my gist. Having spies in your camp will mess your NC up and give your Narc power and avenues into your life that they do not have a right to.

"Being the odd one out, means that you don't fit in with the narcissist's flock of sheep. That's a good thing."

L.W. Hawksby

This space is for you.

Tip 5

Socials Have To Go Bye Bye.

Working forwards from the previous tip, your social media will most likely be a huge part of your past with your Narc. You get Narcs who (claim to) hate social media and are not on it alone or with you, and you get more Narcs who are all over it like jam on toast.

You know which type your Narc is. Although you may have discovered that the person who hated social media is actually a huge fan and knows the emoji catalogue by heart.

Make your own judgement.

But I have to say social media is an ideal place for you to accidentally break NC. Sober, drunk, high, or just in tatters after watching *Love Actually*, or horny, you will turn to social media to fake being happy, post sexy selfies, cry, rage, rant, stalk, message yadda yadda your Narc or people your Narc knows etc.

It is not remotely safe for you when you are in the early stages of NC and trying to heal.

Social media is also a hotbed of gossip, and your Narc will almost certainly be smearing you and blaming you and rallying his/her Flying Monkeys to do the same. Chances are your friends will "warn you" of stuff they see, or you will happen across some of it. You will absolutely feel overwhelming urges to break NC and either unblock the Narc or message them or post about them. DO NOT DO THIS. (I did and it sealed the coffin on my life and resulted in my first criminal conviction. My books cover this.)

Take away temptation and come off social media for the first raw and fragile weeks of NC. Please. Use that time to catch up on what the Narc took from you. Your hobbies, the gym, clothes shopping, cooking, eating, sleeping, those books and those boxsets, holiday planning and friendships. You will detox from socials. But where socials are, your Narc will be, or they will have other people – especially if they know you are into socials!

Surprise and shock your abuser by doing the opposite of what they expect. The highest quality NC ever, pure telecommunications silence.

Use the space below to write down your socials, your handles, your password hints, and new names you are going to use when you "go back" to it. If you go back, that is! Never ever just stay "the same" on socials after and during an NPD abuse break up. You want to make your future Narc-free, so using a different name, handle, hashtag and pic is a great way to move forward, and it's a safer NC-friendly way, too.

"Narcissists hunt to feed.
Psychopaths hunt to kill.
Sadists hunt to enjoy your agony.
Machiavellians hunt to look good."

L.W. Hawksby

This space is for you.

Tip 6

Close All The Windows And Doors.

So, this is something a lot of people (including me) know little about when it comes to NC. And you can absolutely be forgiven for it! You are in the midst of trauma and recovery and all sorts of messes in and around you, so you're not exactly going to be super-vigilant and organised about the opportunities your Narc may take advantage of right now.

No Contact is a simple and smart way to silence the Narc and stop the abuse in many cases. This is true. But Narcs are determined, dogged, persistent, and hungry. Their very personality is all about winning and feeling safe and being fed.

When a supply, aka victim, leaves them (or lets the Narc dump them without too much fuss) the Narc will feel abandoned and lost and utterly hateful. They believe/feel that the only way for their (self-made) pain to end is to get the victim back in some capacity, to feed from them again, and be THE ONE to dump them, but with even more drama (also supply) than on the previous occasion. To win back a victim who knows they are a victim and re-traumatise them is, to a Narc, the ultimate high.

Consciously and subconsciously, a Narc simply HAS to get you back, even if it is to simply have a text exchange or make you feel upset or apologise!

The Narc will do and say anything, anything for this high. For this win. For this power. For the satisfaction of this incredibly dark memory. So you must close EVERY window or door a Narc can use.

Yes, you have blocked the Narc on FB, Insta, Snapchat and

Twitter. I bloody hope so! But there are many other ways that the Narc can still get "in" to your steadily developing house of recovery.

You know your Narc very well. I know Narcs in general very well. So let's work out some ways he or she can get inside your head and your life, that maybe you haven't shut off yet. Yes, what I am really talking about is preventing your own stalking, but Narcs are dark, and this is what they almost always do.

Here are five suggestions to protect yourself from random Hoovering and temptations to break NC and, of course, you can use the space below to write more.

1. Avoid social places you liked together, such as bars, clubs, and restaurants.

2. Do not have your google maps on and do not review places you go.

3. Mess up your routines. If you used to jog every morning along a certain route at 7, change your route and the time you leave the house. Same with dog-walking or work routines or childcare routines.

4. Do not answer calls, texts, emails, DMs etc from your Narcs friends or family and ignore withheld or silent or secret calls and contact too. It is either the Narc or the new supply.

5. Respond calmly and appropriately (and do not respond online) to any false allegations made about you.

This space is for you.

Tip 7

Destroy All Hope.

Hope is something a Narcissistic abuser plays with as though it were a favourite toy. They will bring it out of their box of tricks again and again, because it works in their abuse game again and again.

This space below is for you to write down YOUR hopes and dreams and plans. Forget the ones you made with the Narc. Sorry, but it is absolutely essential.

Narcs will manifest what is called "Future Faking" in the Love Bombing and Hoovering stages before and during the Devaluation stages. They will also whip out fantasies of a "future" with you, and individual plans, when Hoovering.

Many of us breach NC because we hear these beautiful promises of "let's start a family", " I looked at a house for us today", "I'm looking at therapy for us", "I know you always wanted a puppy sooooo...", "I ended it with her, she was our problem and now she's gone", "I re-started my AA recovery yesterday", "I have the money I owe you and want to talk", and "I'm getting a new job and have started saving for our travelling plans!" crap. And, of course, you can scratch down here any other lies you have heard!

Narcs are not imaginative. They will repeat certain promises over and over again. The easy wins. The ones we want oh so so so much!

So, let's have you write down (as many as you like) the ones he/she used most and HOW MANY TIMES you guestimate they said this and, of course, failed!

Once you realise there is NO HOPE for these promises ever coming to fruition, you will find that your Narc is simply a fricking liar. And you will find NC that bit easier again. You won't break it seeking these promises, and you won't believe your Narc when they start spouting them again.

This space is for you.

Tip 8

Flying monkeys, Enablers and Snakes.

Narcissists always have an element of fake altruism and sociability. By this, I mean that they force themselves or, actually, enjoy (depending on the type of Narc they are) being around other people who enjoy being around them because of this false sense of fun and empathy.

Yes, you do get the very "apparently shy" Narcs, but these are really just Narcs who cannot control their impulses and dislike being seen for what they are that often. They will retreat and claim to not like people but still need them for supply, of course.

But most Narcissists will have a social standing and group of supporters, watchers and enablers (I have recorded several videos on this on my YouTube channel – details at the back of this book) who will happily and easily become a Snake for the Narc.

These sneaky, fork-tongued, silent assassins are also called Flying Monkeys, but Snakes are more impotent and passive and watchful and gossipy. Flying Monkeys tend to be active participants (and obvious ones, at that!) in your demise and the Narc's smear campaign and poor me, poor me wailing.

So the Snakes around your Narc are very very discreet, hidden even! They will decide that they are helping the Narc by sliding and hissing into your socials, DMs and phone. They will pretend to care about you, and pretend to want to hear your side.

You will be surprised at who slithers around your neck and starts to seduce you into sharing! You will be hurt, shocked, humiliated, and triggered. This will affect you badly and you will feel intense urges to break NC in the many ways I've already mentioned.

The Narc wants this. They want this from you, just as much as you want now to lose your temper and have the last word! You both WANT to explode! But you are more powerful. You are in control. You hold the power. You are recovering. You are beyond the Narc's worst nightmares. You are going to sniff the Snakes out early on. You are going to block and ignore any that you let in and then realise are not talking to you for authentic reasons.

Look out for random people friending, following, subscribing and DMing you.

Look out for the "Hi! Are you ok! What happened!?" contact from people who never helped you when you were IN the relationship.

Look out for the "Did you know..." and "Have you heard..." type of people. They are just enjoying the bloodbath and being a part of it. Maybe even trying to win points for telling you nasty stuff about your Narc, that really has no positive influence on you right now.

Look out for the "I don't know why this happened! You seemed so happy!" crap too. These people are vultures. They want to see and eat the guts of what happened, and you will not only never hear from them again, but they will also share what you share with you-know-who!

Listen to your instincts. You are in pain. What sort of normal, decent, useful person acts like you are ready to talk and share and bitch and moan, just so they can go back to watching *The Bachelor* or *Strictly* right after triggering you and getting all the goss?

This space is for you.

Tip 9

Guts And Instincts.

Being in a relationship with a true Narcissist, love (or admiration!) really is blind. But we don't put the Stevie Wonders on, the Narc does.

For a Narc to really get full supply, for as long as they want it, from a victim, they need the victim pretty much numb, dumb and spaced out from what is occurring to and around them. This is often called "The Mind Fog" and it is you ignoring or rose-tinting things your Narc does that (deep down you know) are wrong.

You can probably think back, and write down when your inner Psychic Sally gave you an elbow to the ribs or made your brain hurt with "Oh dear, this doesn't feel right"-type feelings and thoughts. Those uncomfortable, tingly, edgy moments of fear and panic and wtf, that you brushed aside because you adored/trusted or were afraid of your Narc. Or the reality of it was just too shocking to cope with, so you chose not to.

In time, your body gives up trying to warn you. And you get better at smothering the warning signs that your gut tries to make you see. Narcs love this. They are all over this. This is THEIR thing. Making you literally stop trusting yourself!

So, let's fight back. Now you are away from that poisonous atmosphere and dream-like Hoovering and future faking, you can start putting your mind to being you again. And a huge part of you is the little inner voice you have. The voice you ignored when your private parts and ego seemed to be louder and more important!

I am particularly empathic, and I also suffer from a very high level of psychic abilities. I lost every single one when I was in the presence of my Narcs. I am utterly mortified that such a special part of me was silenced by the people who deserved less than a minute of my time.

But I have picked up self-awareness and trust in The Universe and my instincts now are better than ever before.

List when you felt that "Oh no" tingle. How it felt. Every detail of it. Explore your instincts and gut feelings. All day, every day, you can work on it and use it and very very rarely will acting on it lead you down the wrong path.

These skills are key in you maintaining your NC. Because when your Narc tries to Hoover you or break NC in any way, you should hear the warning bells and feel the clench in your gut that represents NOOOOOOO and not "Oh, go on then"!

Trust yourself. You know right and wrong, and you know safe and unsafe. I promise.

"Self-love is Kryptonite to toxic people."

L.W. Hawksby

This space is for you.

Tip 10

No Mercy.

Firstly, when we are with an abuser such as a Narcissist, we live and breathe hope that they have the same level of empathy and willingness to change and be a better person each day, as we do. It takes far too long for most of us victims to realise that we are in the movie *Groundhog Day*, and our abuser will not change.

From this point, we are wrestling with horrific disappointment (which can at least eventually lead to acceptance) and wrangling with the all-too-human urge to forgive our abuser for what they have done or are doing. We want desperately to be able to forgive and have mercy because we think that showing such stark humanity must (must!) must surely flick a switch in the abuser and "make" them change, just for us.

So we start to con ourselves and fixate on mercy for our abuser. We will go over and over what (alleged) terrible experiences our Narc says "made them this way". The abuser will have told some truth, told lots of lies, and certainly vastly exaggerated their childhood trauma, ready for today. Ready to get you all forgiving and merciful, ready to abuse you all over again.

Secondly, society has a thing about forgiveness, doesn't it? Whether you are religious, spiritual, or have just been brought up well, you will think you HAVE to forgive anyone who wrongs you, so you can be a good person, and move on.

If you refuse to forgive or can't, it is highly likely an awful lot of people will frown and sniff and question your kindness. These people are almost always those who have never been involved with a Narcissist and have probably never been repeatedly abused by someone who is supposed to love them. Ignore them. Ignore anyone judging you while you struggle with forgiving someone who (right now, in these early days of No Contact) does not deserve it.

This space is for you.

Tip 11

Forgiveness Is Not Your Friend.

Forgiving a Narcissist while you are still trying to apply and maintain No Contact, is a dangerous move. You may be confusing feelings of Trauma Bond with forgiveness and trying to make excuses to go back and "help" the Narcissist, all the while putting yourself back in harm's way. The number of times I have heard "I am a good person. I'm going to try again. He/she needs forgiveness and then we can start afresh" only to have the victim back in contact with me a few weeks or months later, doubly broken that they opened up an already scarred heart, to someone who just wanted to pour vinegar in the wound.

But do you want to be merciful? Well, here's the thing; being merciful to a Narcissist can happen remotely. You do NOT need to break No Contact AT ALL to forgive or feel mercy. You can pray for your abuser, and you can hope for the best for them, and you can let the rage and disappointment go. All without actually picking up the phone, unblocking the Narc on social media, or asking a friend to pass a message on!

This space is for you.

Tip 12

Find Your Marty McFly.

By this I mean, let's go back in time. Fast! As soon as you start considering those little edgy and ticklish ideas of checking your Narc out online, or unblocking, you need to drag your rose-tinted backside backwards, super-duper fast. Get real.

"He must love me, he's unblocked me" and, "She said she loved me so much, she couldn't be with me" – this kinda stuff is what we victims soak ourselves in, and start to drown. We want to believe the idealization and love bombing and previous Hoovering phases meant we were truly loved and respected.

Even if your abuser said 100 lovely things recently (when trying to get you to break No Contact for example) it is irrelevant, compared to the one horrendous thing they said or did.

The past abuses are fact. The present compliments and promises are fiction. Stay in this zone, stick with what the Narc did, and not what the Narc is future faking on and saying they will do.

This space is for you.

Tip 13

Co-dependency Or Wanting To Be Loved?

This chapter was originally just about co-dependency. But, on reflection, I have to be respectful to the few abuse victims (who return to the abuse contexts over and over again) who may not be co-dep. They may simply be "just" Trauma Bonded, or left with no other financial or parental option other than to go back and break NC.

However, I urge you to please, please, read up on signs of co-dependency. And consider if you tick any of those boxes. It is not a shameful thing or a dirty word, and I feel a lot of other experts and advocates seem to think being co-dependent is some sort of insult. It is not.

Co-dependency forms because we were not taught healthy dependency on other people. That is not our fault. However, recognising how it plays a part in our management of abusive contexts and our decisions to return to them can be our responsibility.

Abusers who are good at being abusers (such as Narcissists) rely on targets and victims having co-dependency issues. This is what keeps us around way longer than we should be. We are the ideal long-term supply. And the longer you are with an abuser, the longer it takes to heal.

If you have not had fair and even relationships in the past, you fawn over close friends, family members and partners to feel safe and needed, and are uncomfortable being on your own to the extent you seek out anyone to have distraction and company, then you are waving quite a few flags for abusers to not just abuse you, but to contact you after a period of absence and Hoover you right back in for more abuse. You will really struggle with No Contact because it feels physically uncomfortable being alone and away from someone you feel you need "no matter what".

My advice here is to do everything you can, alone. Painful? Agitating? Exposing? Confronting? Yes. But it is far far better than feeling lost, sad, confused and angry at the hands of someone else.

It doesn't take long for you to recalibrate your dependency levels and feel peaceful rather than lonely, comfortable rather than anxious, and chilled out rather than worried. Give it a few weeks and when you are suddenly around someone who triggers your co-dependency, you will feel it starkly and step away. These people (new to you or your Narc) will upset your newfound equilibrium and you will step away swift and smart, and No Contact will feel sweet, instead of unsteady.

To finish, I have to say I feel no one was as co-dependent as me! Omg, I would obsess over making contact with the most horrid of people, and always made that first call to my Narc mum and certainly felt that without my Narcs I somehow didn't exist. Flaming dangerous!

The Covid Lockdowns ensured I lost a very busy (alcohol-focused) social life, and this removed my crutch. On my own at home, or in my garden, I itched for companionship. I hit lows in my mood and motivation to do anything, and spiked highs in my anxiety beyond anything I had seen. I realised I needed other adults close to me, to feel like I was alive and that if I wasn't having sex, fawning or caring for someone (far too deeply) I felt hollow and, in the shadows of those empty spaces, low self-esteem and boredom lurked. This was a revelation! I now knew my biggest driver for harassing people who had hurt me into being around me, was as a result of my co-dependency.

In the end, I went 18 months pretty much just me. Yes, I had my kids, but my co-dependency plays out worst with adults and even worse with intimate partners. So I was forced to sit and simply... be.

I detoxed from bad people. I learned about myself. I started to re-learn how to be me without needing other people to do so. I had cause to create No Contact with two men online (not known to each other) who were clearly using women's forced isolation to hunt victims.

Neither man got near my heart or soul. As soon as I felt myself start to get too intense, to fawn or be triggered by their avoidant and grooming behaviours, I gave them a telling-off and blocked them, and the only person breaching No Contact was them. And I enjoyed ignoring them.

Had I not done "the work" on my co-dependency, I would have fallen into relationships with these males (not at the same time!) and had months of abuse instead of a couple of hours of red flags.

This space is for you.

Tip 14

The Grass Being Greener.

A toxic person, such as a Narcissist, will preach and boast and message and post all over social media (or more discreetly brag to people they know you are in touch with) about how amazing their life without you is and often they add in extra salt to your wounds, with yelps of joy and picture-perfect joint-selfies. Chuck on the inevitable memes shared between the Narc and anyone who they deem as supportive, and you as the Victim (and ex-partner or ex-friend etc) are filled with a triggering combination of envy, regret, guilt, jealousy and panic that you've done the wrong thing by ending the relationship and going NC.

Stop! Yes, it LOOKS like the Grass Is Greener over there now you've left the Garden, but it is yet more taunting, baiting, pretence and gaslighting. All this over-the-top showing off is for your benefit. The Narc and his new supply are doing it for different reasons.

1. The Narc knows you well enough, and knows their craft well enough, that these public displays of their new relationship and plans for the future will hurt you and either trigger you into breaking NC to have a go at the Narc OR try to reverse the Narc back so you can be in on this lovely new life.

2. The Narc knows you are watching. It is extremely rare for victims to go NC and not look at the Narc's social media or ask around about them when we are in the early days of the break-up or when we are feeling vulnerable or lonely. So when you are seeing all this

stuff, you are seeing what the Narc wants you to see. Aka, not the truth.

3. The Narc's new supply is an unwitting Flying Monkey and Enabler of this charade. She/he will absolutely love being tagged in posts and sharing pictures about the new relationship. They will be insecure about any ex of the Narc because the Narc will have those best-laid plans as soon as possible with a new victim.

4. The Narc knows how to puppeteer everyone on their pages. They know there will be a lot of oohing and aahing and congratulations and false delight at the new relationship that seems so much better than the old one with you. It's easy to applaud a person glorying a new partner as the love of their life, or best friend ever etc. All it takes is a like and a cute emoji. It is not REAL SUPPORT. It is support for what is not real, either by people who are glad you split (Flying Monkeys and other Narcs in your Narc's life) or people who have zero idea what really went on and never will. All this support and celebration is more layers of glass to the life of mirrors you are now coming to realise the Narc built around you, before the real abuse started.

Understanding and using this knowledge should help you see the wood for the trees here, and not that the grass is greener after all. Top Tip: Remember NPDs cannot change. They cannot suddenly turn into a romantic, loving, loyal, kind, and passionate person just because they met someone new. It's all just Love Bombing, just like you experienced. And it will soon turn to regular splits, pics being deleted, tearful begging memes and posts on the new victim's socials, just like it does with most NPD abuse victims who are into social media.

Stop looking. Stop stalking the Narc and the new supply's pages. Detox cold turkey from this poison.

This space is for you.

Tip 15

Hashtag It.

I've put this tip right in the middle of this guidebook so you can't miss it!

Reading other people's success stories of maintaining No Contact was helpful for me, and I suggest it can really help you, too. Please add your own tips and success story for maintaining No Contact. Using the hashtag NoContactNoNarc, I'd like to create a community of people who have read this and are finding it useful.

I set up #NoContactNoNarc as soon as I started writing this book.

This space is for you.

Tip 16

Attraction Schema.

This tip is really about suggesting you do two things to help you stay No Contact with your Narc.

1. Researching something called Attraction Schema.

2. Looking back (honestly) about when and how your Attraction Schema formed its first roots in your psyche.

In brief, Attraction Schema is when we feel (what we think is) sexual or platonic attraction to someone who subconsciously reminds us of a person who hurt us in childhood at an important stage of our emotional and social development. Consciously we (think) we feel a fizz of desire or this deep draw to fun and someone we feel an innate affinity with.

We will often replicate our parents' or caregivers' dysfunctional (or abusive/unfaithful) relationships in our own adult lives and have absolutely no idea we are doing so, until we start to log who we think we love/fancy/are drawn to and how we behave towards them, and what we take from them and put up with.

Looking carefully, we are mirroring relationships we saw as young people, and are trying to fix them now in adulthood. But we are not fixing them because we are drawn to people who cannot or do not want to be fixed. We do not know how to stop these cycles or understand that magnetic draw we have to certain individuals who only seem to disappoint or hurt us.

My tip here is that you note down – here or wherever you want – what dynamics you think you are replicating. Who did you really care for and trust who let you down with how they behaved in a relationship? When did you feel you needed to help or protect someone? And is that anything familiar in the people you now seek out or are drawn to?

Once we recognise that buzz is actually a schema and we are just about to head into the same old crap again, we can stop the bus and back away long before we have even bonded to the person making us feel excited, high or aroused.

And if we are trying to stay No Contact with someone who has flared (and taken advantage of) our Attraction Schema, and see that the fizz and buzz of soulmates is really adrenalin and inner-gut alarms of "Run!", we can recognise the danger and not give in to what we think is a soulmate or twin flame nonsense. Those feelings are danger, danger, danger, run away. Not go, go, go run to!

This space is for you.

Tip 17

Going No Contact with Your Former Self.

This tip was inspired by a tweet I saw, and has been amalgamated into a tip I was going to do, but felt it was a bit rough and ready and could be interpreted as victim-shaming by anyone not ready to face the facts of how they came to be a victim of an abuser such as a Narc.

In all honesty, you know you ignored some red flags at the start of the relationship. The fast pace, the excessive compliments, the fanciful promises of a dream life together, for example. Narcissists will idealize you and the relationship with you, consciously and sub-consciously, and play on weaknesses you have.

Those weaknesses can be your enjoyment of flattery, and interest in some sort of dream lifestyle, for example. Or maybe you have a thing about White Knights or Princesses, depending on your taste for partners! At the end of the day, our willingness to be seduced by what are essentially words (and if you're lucky) gifts and excitement, is a flaw. Call it being shallow or call it having low self-esteem, there is no importance in what anyone calls it. Narcs sense this and boom, we are targeted on the cheap, and fast too!

Going No Contact with who you were before, is a pretty good idea! A lot of victims aiming to be survivors say they wish they could go back to who they were before, and my advice is always "No, you don't"!

Those of us who not only maintain NC and break the cycle of abuse are keen to shed who we were and become less easily led, less easily flattered and more aware of the difference between authentic, thoughtful, charm and seductive, grooming, predation. How we FEEL when we are being idealized (aka targeted) and charmed (aka seduced) is a key indicator of what route the relationship will take.

When a Narc tries to Hoover you with all the crap you heard in the Idealisation and Love Bombing phase (and you haven't even replied yet), you will be repelled by the snake-like flattery and pushy content. In the past, the old you fell for it. These feelings of distaste are damn' helpful in maintaining No Contact!

And in future relationships, the new you will spot predatory and grooming language a mile off, thus breaking the cycle and helping you grow your self-awareness and resilience in the long term.

Go No Contact with the old you. Feel free to scribble here some of the promises and flattery you fell for. And how you felt. Reading it will help you see where you can make changes and never break NC off the back of those changes.

Lastly, I fell for pure seduction with both my Narcs. Not a present. Not a gift. Nothing. Just words and promises, and my shallowness and desire for the perfect relationship and a perfect future, got me almost a decade of abuse. Never again.

"I would rather be a wolf, than a wolf in sheep's clothing."

L.W. Hawksby

This space is for you.

Tip 18

Good Influences

This is something that really worked for me and some of my closest friends as we worked through and sustained No Contact together. We made sure we were around each other and that we were all aiming for the same thing, and would all tell each other the truth and do the work to maintain No Contact.

We were accountable to each other and ourselves. We wanted to be proud of each other and ourselves. And we did not ever encourage each other to do anything that could even slightly reduce our resilience or boundaries in NC.

Be around people who have aspirations and ambitions and good mental health, and who believe in love and loyalty. To see true love and true friendship, and people who stand up for themselves and have boundaries, was a huge thing for me.

I saw how much this made their lives better, and that my choices to be around toxic and abusive people who had no boundaries and plans for the future was too risky for me.

Abuse victims often flock to each other, but really you need to surround yourself with survivors and people you want to emulate.

This space is for you.

Tip 19

Phone A Friend.

This is one you will have done, but maybe in the wrong way! When we are in abusive relationships where most of the abuse (if not all) is psychological and we can't quite put our finger on it being actual Domestic Abuse (it is, by the way) we often feel comfortable sharing the events with close friends, maybe even colleagues, family members and perhaps the abuser's circle too. I don't know about you, but I am a super-over-sharer! And I think Narcs often target communicative and open people, especially for intimate relationships. If we are talkers, we give lots of supply to a Narc who will absorb all that attention, analytical thinking, and honesty, and eat it up like Jelly and Ice-cream.

Anyway, back to the advice on how to use friends to stabilise and maintain your No Contact, instead of using them as a shoulder to cry on, and as emotional support people.

Ah, see! I led you down that path quickly, didn't I? Has it just hit you that you have offloaded to your people perhaps a little too much? Repeated the same worries, woes, and cycles of shock, grief, anger, going back, that abusers like us to do? Your friends have been through it with you and, to a certain extent, you have probably been a bit of a pain in the ass.

Repetitive abuse and Trauma Bonds mean we will play this out with our people and drain them, and yet ignore the advice to stay away (going No Contact) and move on. You ignored your people's advice, didn't you? A lot. You frustrated them and maybe even lost friends? Yes? And maybe you were drawn to new people who said what you wanted to hear and helped you have contact with your abuser and fix the (so-called) break-ups.

Well, all that's gotta stop now. It's time to invest in your real friends and ask for help to stay No Contact. Real friends will back you all the way. Fake ones will quickly become bored. The ones associated with your Narc will try to sabotage your NC – be careful of those.

So, you've chosen your people anew. The close circle you trust who saw the Narc before you did and who won't let you go back and who has your back. Good. These people can do these things for you.

1. Take your phone from you as soon as you start the actions of unblocking or calling or texting or stalking your Narc's pages.

2. Change your password and give it back to you when you've calmed down or sobered up!

3. Won't let you drink or drug alone when you've had a few days of feeling weak and considering breaking NC. Or they won't let you consume any chemicals at all. When in early NC, and still Trauma Bonded, it's best (but not easy) to stay away from anything that will loosen your boundaries and have you getting all upset and breaching the carefully constructed NC you've been working so hard on

4. Remind you of what you have to lose by breaking NC.

5. Remind you (brutally) of what the Narc did to you.

6. Remind you that you are worthy of a decent loyal human being in your life, and that you are a

God/Goddess and not a victim anymore.

7. Distract you with anything, to take your attention from communicating with the Narc. Whatever works, do it. For me, it was filling the freezer with lasagnas, cakes, pies, and curries. Or playing pool for hours on end. A bit of healthy competition and a chance at beating my pool partner was always better than sending a rant to my Narc!

8. Give you an ultimatum. I know this might not be what you want to hear. But a good friend will back away from you if you are determined to keep breaking NC and then go and complain to them when the cycle of abuse continues. You may well love your friend more than you love your abuser, so a little warning of maybe losing your friend might force your hand in maintaining NC in weak moments.

I lost pretty much all my friends when I was with my Narcs. Lots of reasons were in play. But the one I can really take responsibility for is that I leaned on my three closest friends far, far too much and they simply had enough of me going back and then leaning on them again, over and over. I was selfish, thoughtless, and weak. Who wants a friend like that? Victim or not?

A final tip I suggest is that you start finding friends who have been through what you are going through. People dedicated to No Contact or Grey Rock will all be supporting each other and will welcome you. You might even find a Sponsor! Someone who is solid NC and happy to answer a DM or call when you are about to breach your NC, who can stop you with a few minutes of time, advice and attention.

This is something I do formally as a No Contact Coach. Talking victims off the ledge, so they can move to being survivors, and getting that message a few weeks later saying they are still NC and feeling stronger than ever, is wonderful. There are lots of people like me on social media who would be only too willing to help you.

This space is for you.

Tip 20

Scare The Narc Into Leaving You Alone

No no no no no! I do not mean a burly pal with a baseball bat or getting a big dog (I did both, do not follow that lead). I mean getting your words in order either alone or with a legal representative. You may only feel (but not do) this if your Narc simply continues harassing or Hoovering or baiting you, and you sense that it won't stop without a friendly reminder of the law.

Stage 1 of this: You email the Narcissist (with read receipt) AND send the same content in a letter that needs to be signed for to prove they received it, ideally on the same date with a trusted witness (such as a best friend, a neighbour, a doctor, lawyer, or similar professional or family member). You say something along these lines.

> *We split up on date:_____for_____*
> *reasons. I do not wish to have any form of contact*
> *with you whatsoever. If you persist in making contact*
> *with me directly in any way, including*
> *telecommunications, letters, social media, or through*
> *third parties such as shared contacts or fake*
> *accounts, I shall consider this contact to be*
> *harassing, stalking and threatening behaviour. Until*
> *such time as I see fit* (here you only see fit to have
> contact if you have shared financials or a child, for
> example), *you are formally advised that any contact*
> *will be reported to the police. They will then act as*
> *they feel necessary, and I will not shy from*
> *supporting them with recordings, screenshots and*
> *witnesses wherever possible.*

Leave me alone. Full stop. End of. It's over. I am done.

If this has no impact or the Narc still breaches the boundaries you have clearly put up here, get a lawyer or solicitor to repeat this message in a formal letter to your Narc's address, his/her solicitor and, possibly, even a workplace or all of these.

You can get Non-Harassment Orders or Non-Molestation Orders or have the police verbally warn a person who won't let you alone. This is where you need to put some direct effort in but omg it really works.

This space is for you.

Tip 21

Triggers & You.

Working out what your activators and triggers are, when you are considering or even breaking No Contact, is essential. In fact, this is not a tip – it is an order!

My activators were alcohol or drugs – one of those has gone and the other one is far better managed! Anything that heightened my emotions of loneliness, and forgiveness, were a risk for me and I'd start thinking about the Narc and the what ifs. Later, as the anger set in, I'd think it was about time my Narc had a piece of my mind (again) and maybe then they'd explain/apologise/give me closure or change. Of course, I was wrong. We all are if we think the abuser will change.

My triggers for thinking about breaking No Contact (for any reason) in the early days would be seeing anything online about them and their new supply and it being all lovey-dovey as it was in the beginning with us. The pain was indescribable, and I would convince myself the pain would only go away if I spoke to the Narc. Sad and misguided. The pain of NPD abuse only gets worse with the Narc around; it only gets better when we stay NC and well away from them.

Silly things like certain songs, smells, and places would also set me off thinking about breaking NC. You just gotta put the work in to avoid these, and then gradually use exposure therapy as you feel stronger. If you love the gym but the smells and sounds just have you obsessing about your Narc and maybe contacting them, or hoping to see them there, you must avoid the gym!

If playing a sad song (or your song) over, and over again, has you sobbing and crying and writhing in pain, blocking and unblocking the Narc, in the vain hope they see you are open to talking, you must stop playing that damn' song! Don't trigger yourself irresponsibly.

If it helps, keep a diary or note down dates and triggers here. You will see a pattern fairly quickly which will help you plan ahead for triggers, and respond appropriately to activators, before you pick up your car keys or phone.

This space is for you.

Tip 22

The No Contact Agenda

No Contact is not a punishment or a game or a way to show your Narc you are serious and fed up this time! I think a lot of victims use No Contact as a sort of warning to an abuser when in the early stages of exploring and applying it. It's a mistake, but I won't beat you up for it. You're gonna feel shizer enough!

I respond to a lot of Quora posts where the original poster has asked why No Contact isn't working. Why the Narc hasn't come back or fixed themselves yet. These posts make me tense up, but then I remember we don't all have experience of these monsters sufficiently to realise that trying to manipulate them with NC is fruitless and only gives the Narc long periods of time to carry on misbehaving, knowing fine well you're gonna break NC because you're doing it wrong.

No Contact is not about the Narc. It's about you. It's about your safety, mental health, future, children, career, and all the other things the NPD abuse has impacted. In using No Contact you are wrapping yourself in armour. You are saying a hard NO to your abuser every single minute of every single day of every single week you stay NC.

If it helps you to know that No is basically a Narc's most hated word, so be it. Use NC to punish and frighten your Narc if it helps you maintain it. A little bit of power and control is good. But remember this is not the authentic reason why the No Contact lifestyle is best advised.

You must not obsess over the Narc while doing NC, and put too much onus on how the NC is making your Narc feel. You must focus on how the NC is making YOU feel. Take note of it. Feel it. Enjoy it. Reframe the No Contact into what it is supposed to be – your freedom to heal, grow and get your life back, Narc-free.

This space is for you.

Tip 23

Breadcrumbing; Say No To Carbs!

So you've gone No Contact, but the Narc is still managing to get a few words in here and there? A DM from a fake account. A text from their sister. A note on your car windscreen. Or an email to that email account you forgot you have.

These are just examples, but they all happen. Once you go NC, a Narc will behave in many ways. They rarely get the message and just eff off. They almost always try some breadcrumbing, especially if you have been susceptible to little compliments and gifts in the past. It probably worked a treat in the Love Bombing phase and after discards, so the Narc will return to these techniques to Hoover you in or get you to breach NC and respond. Remember, any response (even anger) is both breaching NC and giving the Narc supply.

You may well be steadfast in not replying to the breadcrumbing. Determined. Stubborn a.f. Laughing at your Narc's pathetic attempts to get you back in their life in some way. Narcs know that eventually they will trigger you or bait you or even wear you down.

You must must must not continue letting this happen. It is not full No Contact if the Narc can make contact with you, in any way. Remove temptation. Remove supply. As soon as you get any hint that your Narc is making contact, delete and block. Don't let it sit there in your inbox or anywhere the Narc knows you can see it and are reading it.

Ignoring this advice is akin to an alcoholic sitting in a bar, watching people drink, and still convincing themselves they will never ever drink again. With enough pressure via breadcrumbing, almost all victims will respond and all the hard work being soberly No Contact is wiped out.

This space is for you.

Tip 24

No Contact Will Make Those Who Love You, Proud of You

Being in an abusive relationship or context absolutely affects the people in our life who care for us. A lot of victims convince themselves that the abuse is well-hidden, that they are strong and doing the right thing by fighting for the relationship etc. I did that myself, and my parents certainly convinced themselves of this.

If you are hurting, people who love you are hurting. It is very simple. Whether they say so or not, or whether you think you are doing your best, is irrelevant. Taking abuse in any form over a period of time will affect you in many ways, often ways you don't appreciate until you are NC and out.

I failed at NC many many times, when I didn't even know I was being domestically abused. I gaslighted myself into allowing the Narc back into my life, head and bed, by saying our relationship was nothing to do with my parenting. But it was. In fact, it destroyed it.

However, I always had one rule. If I ever truly felt my children were directly unsafe/at risk in any situation my Narc manifested, I would leave the relationship. The inevitable happened in February 2016 and my decision was made.

In the end, what helped me stay No Contact was remembering, over and over again, the horror of a particular situation my kids probably remember, and I wanted that to be the last. I saw how dangerous my Narc and his behaviour was, and how weak I was letting it carry on, even with my kids around, and the self-hate and shame kept me NC once and for all.

I suggest you consider how your Narc is impacting the people around you, and important things such as your career and health too. If you can't do NC for yourself (because you are Trauma Bonded, have low self-esteem and feel like you can't cope without your abuser) then do it for people far more important than the Narc. The people relying on you who truly love and need you. The ones who are not abusers or cheats.

Fill in here "I am starting No Contact and Maintaining No Contact for… … …" And in time this list will get longer, and I hope soon your name is on this list in big, bold, letters.

This space is for you.

Tip 25

No Contact And The Mind Fog Are Very Good Friends

I'm not gonna get all fancy here and start talking at you about what the Mind Fog is in Psychiatry or Therapy terms. This guidebook is not written by a PhD, it is written by me. And I felt the Mind Fog starkly and have felt it lift. I have spoken to hundreds of victims who became survivors after the Mind Fog lifted.

The thing is, it only lifts once you remove what is fogging you. And what is fogging you is the trauma of the abuse, the shock of the abuse, the memories of the abuse, and your continued contact with the abuser.

Your mind is incredible. While you have been suffering the most extensive and varied psychological attacks on your sense of self, morality, instincts and mental health, your brain has moved to protect you from it getting so deep you are never coming back. Your brain has literally fogged out a huge amount of feelings and perceptions of reality, and kept it under control so you can face it when you are ready. When the perceived threat (aka the abuser) is gone.

So you have been wrapped up in a blanket of denial and cognitive dissonance until now. Until the day you decide No Contact is essential for your survival and recovery. Hours into your staying away from the abuser, the Mind Fog starts to gently, slowly, dissipate.

Pennies will drop (you know the saying, right?), memories will resurface, and you might start having flashbacks and dreams too. Do not be afraid. Do not fight it. These have all sat behind the Mind Fog until you allowed them in. And you need to allow them in.

As it gradually dawns on you how hard your body has worked to protect you, and how much has really been going on while you have been fighting to love your abuser, things change. It can feel uncontrollable and terrifying and shocking, and shame and guilt and remorse will creep in.

These feelings are your friends. The memories and realisations are, too. Write them down, tell your people, and ruminate on them. You are quite seeing the light, and in that light is your freedom.

No Contact will feel like a safe place now. And it is your weapon against more abuse and your newfound best friend for any future red flags or abuse events.

This space is for you.

Tip 26

If Shit Hits The Fan, You Can Prove You Wanted No Contact When You Get The Knock

This is an important one! Narcissists are master manipulators and will not hesitate to wreak havoc when they realise you are NC, and always will be. Whatever their reasoning, they will almost always wrap a big victim cloak around themselves, and tell anyone and everyone who listens that YOU are harassing them and ruining THEIR No Contact. Yup – it's a thing they do. And if they don't cry wolf on this, there are an awful lot of Flying Monkeys and Narcissistic Supplies who will sing this song too.

So being No Contact in itself will protect you from these false allegations. Narcissists love using police, social care and other public sector organisations (and even domestic abuse and stalking charities!) to harass you. By harassing, I mean upsetting you. Labelling you. And blaming you for whatever pain or shame or fear (yadda yadda) the Narcissist says you are causing.

If you have maintained No Contact, blocked the Narc everywhere and do as many of the things I suggest, you will have proof of your innocence when these allegations occur. At the end of the day, Narcissists will do ANYTHING to play the victim and cause a true victim trauma. Yes, it will be upsetting and stressful to have a call or knock at the door from (for example) a police officer, saying your ex-Narc has reported you for (for example) repeatedly texting the Narc or posting online about them, but true No Contact disallows those actions so you should have nothing to worry about.

A Narc can twist one simple text, saying "Leave me alone, you horrible person" and let you call them once, twice, three times (and not answer) and boom, you are harassing them. You have breached No Contact and put yourself right into the Narc's hands in doing so. Narcs are known for begging you to contact them, and then reporting you when you do!

So the tip is to always fear that false allegation of telecommunications harassment! It is not worth the risk in having any contact with a Narcissist, just in case they do decide to destroy your life because you wanted to have a chat or try to get closure. When you feel the itch of neediness, and glance at your phone, thinking "one voicemail message" won't hurt, remember it really can!

Imagine the pride you will feel (and the sense of safety!) when you can calmly sit down with whoever is accusing you of harassing your Narc, when you show them your phone and laptop and can prove you created and maintained NC yourself, by changing your number, changing your email, blocking the Narc everywhere and not having called or texted since you began your road to recovery! Delish!

The Narc will be sniffed at and shamed by their nasty dangerous false allegation and be forced to start their own road to bloody well leaving you alone!

"The tide goes in and out. Flowers bloom and wilt. The sun shines, then sleeps. As you heal from narcissistic abuse, you will feel the ebb and flow of it."

L.W. Hawksby

This space is for you.

Tip 27

Your Own Self-esteem? How's That?

Right. So let's check-in! If you remember, it is rare as hen's teeth for your Narc to ask (genuinely) how you are. Yeah, they might eye you closely, or send a bland "How are you?" or even put an arm around you and ask if you're ok but, take it from me, this is neither authentic nor empathic. This abuser and cheat is simply saying what they think they should say and pretty much conning you into thinking they really do care about your wellbeing, mental health status, and self-esteem.

Now is your time to focus on yourself. And your self-esteem is a bloody good place to start! This section of the book has three parts, and three parts for good reason.

1. Check in on yourself regularly. By doing this you are taking focus from thoughts of the Narc and placing them where they should be. On yourself!

2. You are keeping an eye on how you are feeling so that when you acknowledge feeling vulnerable, lonely, sexually frustrated, tired and in need of a cuddle etc etc, you are owning it and can work on it, instead of giving in to it and breaking No Contact with your Narc. You might want to consider noting down how you feel in this book, and think closely about how to self-soothe healthily with no Narc involvement. Keeping yourself aware of yourself will help you stay No Contact, and build self-awareness and resilience.

3. Do not (and I mean it!) post anything online or tell

anyone you do not 100% trust is not your Narc's Flying Monkey, which could be construed as being or feeling open to comfort. Your Narc will see or hear this and immediately either celebrate (horrible twat that they are) or use it to plan a way to contact you or wobble your hard-earned boundaries.

This space is for you.

Tip 28

Be Discreet

Once back on social media, you must know that a Narcissist (who has been waiting for you and watching for you and desperate for your availability) will know almost immediately that you are "back".

They will perceive this in their typically warped world as you now needing them again. Narcissists are delusional. They are as delusional as they make us! They believe your presence back in their area/at their pub/on social media or even walking past them in the street is you needing them and making yourself known to them.

So, here is a banger of a tip. BE DISCREET. Everything you post now, forever, online (as it should have been before) must be vague, without defining characteristics, and discreet. You can disclose that you're in a new relationship but do not share the new partner's name. You can disclose being on holiday, but do not share where! I actually use a time-delay technique. I post really fab stuff several days after it happened so my Narc feels no involvement or hold over me. He was not there when I posted my next book release. He was not there when I was canal-boating. He was not there when I changed my hair.

Narcs feel involved if we let them. Crazy? Yes. But it is good solid pure No Contact to be as discreet as you can. Soon, you get a bit of a rise from it. I know I do.

This space is for you.

Tip 29

Remember The Pain

A lot of NPD abuse survivors get to a point of feeling almost cocky with how far they've come. And to be fair, we should be darn' proud to have almost completely annihilated that Trauma Bond, deleted the Narc's everything, not reacted to baiting or Hoovering or done anything that could be defined as breaking our NC.

This can be a dangerous time. Why? Because we might lose focus on NC and, much like an addict who has been clean and sober for a year, and dares to take a sip of beer, a person doing NC can slip and think that now is the time to have that "final coffee date" or respond to that Happy New Year gif the Narc sent.

No, no, no! I have coached a few people who thought they were strong enough and, lo and behold, they were again seduced by the Narc and, at best, felt horrid for weeks after, because the Narc triggered them badly or, at worst, they slept with the Narc. You cannot understand how devastated these people were when they realised that they had (their words, not mine) "ruined their recovery and gone back to ground zero".

The only way to maintain NC is to understand NC is like sobriety; it must be a lifetime commitment. You have been through extreme, mind-altering trauma and there will always be something between you and your Narc. Even if you hate every cell in their body and wish they were in a shallow grave somewhere, having any contact with them where you hear their voice or see their face will drag you backwards and give your healing body the fright of its life.

Narcs also find great, great pleasure (supply) in a healed victim, who is now considered a survivor, saying yes to that benign, innocent "just as friends" coffee date, or other very small breaches of NC. A breach is a breach. And contact is contact.

You must must must not think you are incapable of being impacted by an "innocent" chat or meeting. You are indeed amazing, but Narcs know how to destroy our new boundaries and feelings of success in an instant. You are a better person than the Narc, but the Narc is a better manipulator, and always will be.

So to stop yourself falling at this last hurdle and sipping that disastrous beer, note down here how you felt after you broke NC the last time. Self-hatred, rage, anxiety, disappointment, shame, etc. These feelings are your friends in maintaining NC once you are coming to the end of your NC process and cementing it in your life for good.

They are not to make you feel bad, they are to REMIND you of what you do not want and what you will get if you let NC be broken now things are "better than ever" in your life. Narcs often pop up when you are almost totally healed. They have a sixth sense for it. And to destroy your NC now, at this point, is one of their favourite things. Many victims don't come back from it.

This space is for you.

Tip 30

Be Aware, Showing Off Your New Love Will Trigger A Narc To Try Even Harder To Smear, Stalk And Hoover You!

So here we are, and you've met someone. (Well, you will one day if you haven't yet!)

A Narc's worst nightmares are being exposed, losing supply that is still fruitful, and a victim sticking to NC and having a wonderful stable happy life after the Narc "failed" to destroy them. To a Narc, your betrayal of moving on is agony. NC also is ridiculously painful. It represents your apathy towards the Narc and oh boy, does that hurt!

So a Narc may well try to break your NC at this point. Most of them do! My Narc2 did, and when I laughed at him and told him to eff off, he flipped and threatened to kill me. Of course, he also threatened suicide and when that also didn't work, he decided that I led him to that and mocked him and got the Police on his side... and that was the start of a whole new level of post-separation abuse that would make even Hannibal Lecter's eyes widen in disbelief.

So, my advice here, to avoid the Narc trying to break NC and avoid you getting all over-excited and sharing your newfound life in love ANYWHERE online or with possible Flying Monkeys, is to simply say nothing. Being happy and in love is a wonderful thing. It is precious. It is possibly your future now. Protect it like it were a child, puppy, or kitten! Nothing good comes of you promoting where you are at in your recovery right now. Nothing.

You will feel urges to be smug and to show off, and that is

natural. People would say it is narcissistic, but they are idiots. You will want to "hurt" your Narc with your new relationship, and that is a bit Narcy to be fair. Healed and recovered is where you are headed, don't be tempted to go back a few months and do anything your Narc did to you.

Hard? Yes! I acted a total twonk doing stuff like that for ages, and it only ever hurt me or my life and gave the Narc the satisfaction that I was still unstable and trying to hurt him. When I realised that he was enjoying me trying to get a good life (in his mind) just to hurt him with it, all my efforts with NC were dashed. He believed I was breaching NC, and that was bad enough to make me think a lot harder about how to maintain it!

So I "flexed" and privatised my life significantly. What a relief it was (and still is!) to be in love, and happy, and not making a fuss of it. No one even knows the initial of my partner's name, or what part of Scotland he lives in, and THAT I can feel smug about.

Feeling safe, and in a kind of silence, means my NC is as solid as a rock. No triggers. No stalking. No harassment. No nasty tweets or other social media posts.

So, there you are, another important tip for you to maintain No Contact.

"You my Darling, are priceless, and The Narcissist cannot afford You!"

L.W. Hawksby

This space is for you.

About The Author

This is a refreshed ATA section because life has really hugely moved on for me since I wrote my first book. It feels inauthentic to just use one of the "old" ATAs.

It's 2023 now, and 10 years since I first met Narc2 and realised Narc1 was an abuser. I'm not going back there to talk about what happened, as you can buy the books.

What I will say is that by using the Grey Rock Method, I have a decent co-parenting context with "Niall" from *Dangerous Normal People* now, and our son is flourishing in High School. My two older boys are enjoying their journeys in young adulthood and, so far, seem to have broken my family curse and have good safe relationships and solid decent friendships. *** *wipes brow with relief and doffs cap to her children in major respect***

I have more books sitting ready to release (next few pages) and, depending on the date this book is released, I may well be sitting on the roof terrace of my house on the island of Crete! Yes, we finally completed the purchase, got the builders in, and got crazy with the Euros! If you are interested in coming to stay as a free guest (if you are an NPD abuse victim) please find me on social media, my podcast or my YouTube Channel as "The Narcissist Hunter" or "The Original No Contact Coach".

I am steadily working towards gaining my Higher National Diploma in Psychology and have officially started coaching people of all genders into a full No Contact lifestyle also. It's not free, but it won't break the bank if you think you need me for a session or two.

Love and Friendship are always close these days, and being able to type that feels good. I am not enmeshed in my partner or co-dependent on my friends. Of course, I still have some unrest (let's call it that) from my Narcs and their Flying Monkeys but, considering how far I've come in the last decade, I'm pretty happy with how life is just now.

I plan on doing a series of "30 Tips To" books, perhaps something around Narcissistic Mothers, or workplace bullies. Please get in touch if you have an idea!

For more info about me, I have nice long bios on my YouTube channel, Quora account, and Amazon author page, so I won't waffle on much more.

Thank you for buying and reading this book – I really hope it's of help. Now I have only one thing to ask. Statistically, only 10% will review a book. I'm looking to change that statistic. Please, please, please could you now go over to Amazon or wherever you bought this book and rate and review it for me so that others can find it, learn from it, and enjoy it, too!

I hope you have found clarity, validation, and comfort from *No Contact No Narc* the book, and that you have a wonderful Narc-free life.

Dangerous Normal People. Understanding Casanova Psychopaths and The Narcissistic Virus

"The book is cleverly constructed in that the narrative is split up into sections and a summary of the behaviours is listed at the end of each section, giving the reader clear definitions of what kind of behaviours have just taken place in the story and in what manner they are toxic. I was gripped as it bore such a similarity to my life situation of late, and despite me having made the move to thoroughly educate myself on this disorder, there were still so many eureka moments where I thought 'Of course! That happened!' and perhaps I had put it down to a 'bad day' or some other lame excuse. I recognised I was in an abusive relationship about a year before I finally discarded them for good. In the meantime, I kept a detailed diary of events, and was able to chart the patterns of behaviour and recognise the roller coaster and start to mentally detach."

Flinty November 2021

"A well-written book about discovering disordered traits in people.
This subject should be taught in an educational setting in order to help people to understand these types of characters exist."

Sue x January 2023

"I am three-quarters of the way through & this book I cannot put down.
Not only is it helping me heal & move on, but I'm having light bulb moments of things I never thought were control or abuse. I've recommended it to friends & to people in the field of counselling / mental health, as I feel they would benefit reading it - to educate themselves from the author's point of view of what she went through. As no one can understand what anyone goes through unless they have gone through it too , or stepped into someone's shoes that has. This book is real / raw / triggering but ultimately a helper to heal & make one aware of dangerous people / narcissists etc."

Fiona June 2022

"This is a brutally honest, deeply personal retelling of one woman's nightmare years at the hands of a narcissistic abuser. From the thrill of the woo and the relentless pursuit to the blissful honeymoon period, all the way through to the mask slipping when a hellish, insidious dynamic is created in the relationship. The author shares a warts and all account of how she found herself in a destructive, co-dependent relationship in a cycle of the extreme highs and lows, gaslighting, infidelity and abuse as well as abandonment and discarding that comes hand in hand with loving a narcissist. Whilst this isn't an easy read, particularly if you've experienced narcissistic abuse, it's a compelling read and one that all young women should arm themselves with to spot the tell-tale early signs. It's worth the £10 for the 22 point checklist at the end, alone.

Lucy writes honestly, even about the things that don't paint her in a particularly great light. That authenticity however means that you can't help like her, feel extreme compassion and understand the thought processes that shaped her circumstances throughout the period of the book.

I've started her fictional work 'The Notch' today which promises to be just as deep and insightful about the issues explored in this book."

Tenacious Lee November 2020

The Notch

"I would definitely recommend this book, a really clever and unusual premise and a compelling and enjoyable read from start to finish."

Dave Laymen Gregson April 2021

"Intriguing supernatural thriller with some laugh-out-loud moments, I absolutely loved it, and highly recommend. I had my copy personally signed so heaven forbid Lucy "accidentally" falls off a mountain it will be worth a fortune."

Mark Cottrell February 2022

"This book was amazing to read.
Easy to follow.
Enjoyed getting to know the depths of each character.
Had me gripped from the beginning!
A must-read if you need an escape!"

TL February 2021

"Loved the book, the storyline, how you cannot really know about someone at first glance! Very interesting how people's minds work when they know what they want!"

Chloe Bradshaw January 2021

The Forgivers Club: Where you can be *dead* honest.

"Wow just wow ... "gripping" is an understatement, "dark" is accurate and "memorable" is promised ... such a gripping dark and won't be forgotten read. The author ensures you are stuck from the first few pages. Very, very good!"

Debbie Fraser June 2021

"Another brilliantly written book. I was taken in straight away, read it all in one sitting (all day!). Lucy writes brutally honest about the events that unfold! I cannot wait to read 'The Notch!' Excellent read."

Joanne Traynor June 2021

"There is no doubt about it, L W Hawksby has a gift for writing a riveting and compelling story. Drawing on much of her own personal experience she has created a wonderful novel that had me gripped from the first couple of pages. I bought this book to take on holiday in a few weeks, but I had a sneaky peek at the first couple of pages and then just couldn't put it down.

It's a dark tale but told with humanity, wit and an important message regarding the decisions we make and why we make them.

I thoroughly enjoyed this book and I can't wait for L W Hawksby's next release. She goes from strength to strength."

Destinoligee June 2021

"I actually picked this up tonight to read a few chapters before bed and it's now 3 am and I just finished it!! A story about how one person can ruin the lives of others by stalking and harassing an entire town. Also, a wonderful tale about Redemption in the most surprising places."

Tracey December 2021

Upcoming books from L.W Hawksby

(look out for the book title hashtags or follow me on Amazon)

Pretty Girls Gone

"Because Sometimes Hearts Are Meant To Be Broken"

A small village set deep into misty Cornish Moors has its traditions and laws. The women are exceptionally beautiful, and the men are unusually domineering. This is Bridgefell, a place where some of the younger females in the community are committing suicide and yet neither the villagers nor Laird and Lady of the Manor seem to have taken notice, nor began to enquire as to why.

Luna, the local gillie and tomboy, has spotted a pattern and can't help but get drawn into the mystery of what's taking place. She's extra-interested because her mother disappeared from the village while Luna was still a baby.

What is beneath the parties, festivals and frivolity that is causing the darkness in innocent girls' hearts? Why is it they want to be gone?

Dead Happy

"When The Only Way Out Is To Die And Live Again"

Patrick: *"Emma looks radiant and relaxed, and yet I'm terrified. My gut hardens in fear, as my bride-to-be glides towards me wrapped in cream satin, It's as if she's just stepped out of a Greek history book. Her white-blonde hair piled up and yet, impossibly, also flying like the ends of whips, curled around her neck and down to the side of her chest. Every single set of eyes in the church is on her. Thank fuck none are on me.*

Emma winks at me, then nods at the minister to start the bridal march. The basement of my bowels rumbles again with the threat of impromptu defecation and Noel, my best man, nudges me and squeezes my elbow in congratulations, as my horrendous grinning future slides down the aisle towards me. The flowers are perfect. Just as she wanted. The music is perfect just as she wanted. And I am the perfect victim. Just as she wanted.

Following on from these releases in 2023 and 2024 will be **CrazyMaker**, **In The Wind**, **Monster In The Bed** and **Echo's Revenge** – please follow me <u>and</u> the book hashtags!

I am the Narcissist Hunter, subscribe to me on Youtube, listen to me on Spotify and podcasters, follow me on Instagram and Twitter, ask me questions on Quora.

L.W. Hawksby

Glossary of Terms

Narcissist; A person with Narcissistic Personality Disorder.

Narcissistic Personality Disorder; A Mental Health Condition in which people have an unreasonably high sense of their own self-importance. They need and seek too much attention and pathologically need people to admire them and bend to their will. People with this personality disorder have low to no empathy and will mask as confident, while riddled with insecurity, fear of abandonment and jealousy.

Flying Monkeys; Slang term for the people a Narcissist uses to stalk, troll, harass and spy on someone close to or recently separated from the Narc.

Discard; The period of time a Narcissist has placed a victim out of their life either using the silent treatment and ignoring, or adding in stonewalling, blocking on social media, creating a "break-up", and ignoring the victim's attempts to communicate or get closure from whatever triggered the Narcissist to manifest a discard.

Narcissistic Supply; The name given to people around the narcissist who enable, empower or fuel the narcissist in any way. Narcissistic Supplies are always people but can be children of the Narc, also. The supply given can be anything from money, to status, to sex, to reputation enhancement, to alibis, to acting as Flying Monkeys.

The Final Discard (also called "The Grand Finale" in some circles); Is a break-up but only remains so if the victim refuses to go back to the relationship. It is ultimately THE break-up from the Narcissist.

The Smear Campaign; What Narcissists, Flying Monkeys and new/old supplies of the Narcissist will engage in to silence and destroy a victim who is trying to speak their truth, recover or get on with their life after it has ended with the Narcissist.

Malignant Narcissist; A Narcissist who tends to be overt in their behaviour with a good deal of sadism in their personality structure.

A Covert Narcissist; A Narcissist who tends to be more covert (sneaky, careful) in their behaviour.

A Narcopath; A Narcissist who stalks, as Psychopathy underpins obsessive, persistent stalking and smearing behaviour.

Reactive Abuse; When a victim of abuse takes so much and then reacts in an abusive or even criminal manner.

(A reminder, if you want to learn 112 terms and abuses that Narcs specialise in, *Dangerous Normal People* is the book for you!)